Most Blessed

The Joy of
Obedience

Lori Polk

ISBN-13: 978-0-9838763-2-8

Printed in the United States of America

Second Edition

Cover design by Jackie Floyd

Author photo by John Hagy

I loved Lori's book. It helped me realize we have to give it all to God and let Him have control, and everything will work for the good in His perfect timing ~ *Debbie K. Irwin*

Reading Lori's book made me feel as if I was taking her spiritual journey with her ~ *Shelley Lewis*

What a wonderful tribute to your Christianity ~ *Elsie*

Lori's book is a great reminder of God's place in my life. I use this daily in my quiet morning time...and as needed! ~ *LouAnn E.*

I couldn't put Lori's book down. I laughed, I cried. It made me take a look at my own life, and I realized what Lori said is true: when you know better, you do better ~ *Stacey Sullivan*

Lori shares her faith well. It is plain that she hopes to bless others on their spiritual journey through areas of struggle and overcoming. And that she does. It is a heart warming and heart-searching book. I consider myself *Most Blessed* by her willingness to share her spiritual growth with open honesty. It adds so much to mine ~ *Jan Golon*

Lori's book is incredibly inspiring. Her captivating insights coupled with simple applications make this book very useful ~ *Patricia Fyffe*

Wow! Your book is a real inspiration ~ *Joyce Riffel*

I can clearly tell by your writings that you have been truly touched by The Holy Spirit and want to share your testimony. We want to embrace your love for Christ so when you share, others will also benefit. I've already been touched ~ *Janet Sandefur*

Lori is a gifted writer. Her wonderful lighthearted approach to obedience in the presence of God is inspiring and simple. I read it from cover to cover in one sitting. Now I am "most blessed" too. Thanks ~ *Barbara Marco*

Your love of Christ is reflected in every page ~ *Mary Anne K.*

It was hard for me to put the book down. I enjoyed each and every page. It is truly a treasure ~ *Ardella*

It is written brilliantly ~ *Terri D.*

Most Blessed made me think of all the things I have been blessed with; a wonderful husband and family, having a wonderful group of friends who love and support me, and best of all, having Jesus Christ in my life who never fails me and gives me the strength to live life to the best that I can ~ *Carmen Kinahan*

Wow!! I just finished Lori's book. It was sooo good – I didn't want it to end!! She is such a good writer – so many profound but simple applications to our lives ~ *Linda Finley*

For Val, Stacey, Michelle & Shelley
My Forever Friends

Table of Contents

Acknowledgments ix

Introduction...xi

Childlike Faith 1

The Divorce 3

From the Frying Pan into the Fire 5

"God On Call" 6

"Take It" 10

Blessings of Obedience 18

Overcoming Addiction 26

Life Principles 27

God's Word—Our Instruction Book.................... 28

The Ways of God 34

Drawing Near to God... 39

Living in the Center of God's Will 41

Fruit of the Spirit 44

Filled with the Holy Spirit 46

Did You Know That…... 49

Prayer and Praise... 53

It's the Everything... 55

Be the One Who…... 60

Our Purpose for Being....................................... 60

The Miracle of God.. 64

Saved by Grace with Love and Mercy 65

Faith... 67

Trust 67

Obedience 68

My Life Today... 68

Let Go, Let God 70

No Bible, No God; Know Bible, Know God 72

May the Lord Bless You and Keep You 72

Acknowledgments

This was written for, and dedicated to, my friends who kept asking me why I'm so happy and smiling all the time. A special "thank you" to Stacey for the constant encouragement and making me believe I could do this. And a "Special Mention" to Pastor Dwight Friesen and Judy Crosby for your thoughtful insights. They were greatly appreciated!

To my sister, Debbie, your words were exactly what I needed to hear. To my dad, Jerry, I always knew I was loved because you not only told me every day but showed me as well. To my mom and dad, Lenie and John, who helped make this book a reality for me. And who also make me feel very loved.

A very special thank you to Sharon K. Souza, my favorite author and mentor, and who I am most blessed to call friend. Thank you for being you!

And especially to my husband, Gary, who has made me the most loved and spoiled wife in the whole wide world, and I love it. I love you mostest.

I know my life wouldn't be this wonderful if my husband didn't go to church. So, thank you Rev. Dr. Alan Kimber, Pastor Dennis Baskin and Pastor Rob Bline, who got Gary loving church. And now Pastor Rod Suess, Vinewood Community Church in Lodi, CA, who keeps him coming back.

And the biggest "THANK YOU" ever to Dr. Charles F. Stanley who taught me how to have my intimate relationship with God. I am eternally grateful to and for you.

Introduction

To me, faith is believing that God is who He says He is; trust is believing that God will do what He says He will do; and obedience is showing God that I have trust and faith in Him. And I do that by giving Him control of every area of my life.

I was tired of the stress, worry, fear and anxiety. Every day of my life. I just wanted it to stop. But how? God came to mind. Often. Fleetingly. Until one day. I was ready. I mean done. Done wanting and needing to control every area of my life. Still, how do I give God control of every area of my life? *Any* area of my life, for that matter. That was the $64,000 question. How to go from believing in God, to walking with God. The obedience part.

I had been watching the First Baptist Church of Atlanta church service called "In Touch" with Dr. Charles F. Stanley for several years. He often said the Bible is our instruction book. So, one day, after hearing it countless times, it finally dawned on me. READ THE BIBLE. To know who God is and who He wants me to be, I needed to read the Bible, again. I had read the Bible before, but only for the stories about Daniel in the lions' den, Job, David and Goliath and many, many more. This time I was going to read it to learn, but I really wasn't sure how the Bible could help me in *my* daily life, it being so old and all. Fortunately, I was wrong and Dr. Stanley was right. The God in the Bible is the same God who lives inside of me. And the awesome things He did for His people back then, He can do for me now. The life lessons, principles and laws were the same yesterday as they are today, except for one huge difference: we don't have to offer sacrifices to God for the forgiveness of our sins. Jesus left His glory and the glory of Heaven to come down and be our sacrificial Lamb, also known as the Lamb of God. He became our sin, the sin of the world. And when they crucified Him on the cross, His shed blood washed *all* of our sins away, *forever*.

This is my journey from believing in God, to having a daily walk with God. Well, at least most days. Because some days….

Childlike Faith

I begin with some background simply to show how life can change in a split second, and how good people can make really bad choices. It's also to show that God doesn't condone the sin, but always, *always* loves the person. You cannot out-sin the grace of God.

I was born to parents who love me very much and told me so every day. I was kissed and hugged on a daily basis and every night my mom would say a prayer with my sister, Debbie, and me. We would say, "Now I lay me down to sleep, I pray the Lord my soul to keep." We would stop there because we didn't want to talk about dying (and that's the next line). Then Mom would sing the song "You are my Special Angel" to us. I knew I was loved, and I felt loved. To this day, every time I get ready to leave my mom's I say, "sing me," and she does.

Every other Saturday my dad would take me to work with him. We always stopped at Helwig's Restaurant for a glazed donut on the way to work. For lunch, we would go across the street to Gaia Delucchi Delicatessen and get a sandwich from Pete. Daddy made things fun, and I don't think he even realized it. We even played football in the street with the boys on the block. Whatever Daddy did, I did. I was Daddy's Girl, and everyone knew it.

We went to Sunday school and church almost every Sunday. I was saved at a young age so I've always known I'm going to Heaven. I learned that God is a Trinity: God the Father, God the Son

(Jesus), and God the Holy Spirit. I never questioned their existence. I had "childlike faith" that the Bible talks about. I also believe John 3:16, "For God so loved the world that He gave His only begotten Son, that whosoever believeth in Him shall not perish, but have everlasting life." That promise from God is how I know, for certain, I'm going to Heaven. I was 26 years old when I found out everyone does not know this verse by heart. I don't ever remember *not* knowing it.

I even survived my baptism. But it was a close call! On baptism day, July 31, 1966, the wall behind the pulpit in our church was opened, revealing the pool of water to the congregation. Those of us to be baptized were off to the side, waiting to be called into the water by Pastor Buhler.

I was watching him put a hanky over the nose and mouth of those going before me, and then laying them backwards into the water. NOT ME!! He's not going to drown *me*! I wrapped myself around my mom's leg and started crying, "No mommy, don't make me do it!" Over and over. I was only six years old and waaaay too young to die. While the Pastor patiently waited, my mom calmed me down, unwrapped me from her leg, and I was baptized. To my great relief I didn't drown.

Growing up I thought every parent told their children they loved them on a daily basis. I also thought everyone believed in God. I was so wrong. I can't imagine growing up in a home without love and where the whole family doesn't believe in God. Unfortunately, that's the reality for far too many.

The Divorce

As a youngster I considered myself a good Christian. I tithed, went to church, and prayed. I was kind to others and always tried to be thoughtful of their feelings. I had a good childhood and by the sixth grade I had my life planned out. When I grew up, I was going to teach first grade and marry Kent. He was the cutest boy in the whole world.

So, you know that old saying, "If you want to make God laugh then tell Him your plans," well, I must keep God in stitches. When I got to high school my counselor told me not to be a teacher. She said there would not be any teaching jobs when I got out of college. That turned out to be the worst advice I ever took. And the cutest boy in the whole world, yeah, he never acknowledged my existence. *Anyway*, since I had never thought of doing anything other than teaching and marrying Kent, I no longer had a plan. There was no Plan B. It never occurred to me to make one. And then there's that other old saying, "Things could always be worse." I don't think I like those old sayings very much.

My sister, Debbie, and I used to babysit for the Hinchmans. One day, Mrs. Hinchman asked us if we could babysit the next day, it was a holiday. We went home and asked mom if we were doing anything as a family, or if we could babysit. Her answer completely blindsided us.

Instead of answering our question she said, "Sit down girls, there's something we need to tell you." We sat and she said, "Your father and I are getting a divorce." WHAT?!?! In complete shock, Debbie and I are like, "No, you can't, we're planning a surprise party for your 20th anniversary!" And less than an hour later, I was waving goodbye to my daddy. Crying uncontrollably. And that's how my life changed in a split second.

Now, at the ripe old age of thirteen, and a freshman in high school, my life is over. No Kent, no teaching job, and now no family. What's a girl to do? Oh, wait, it gets better. The night before my parents announced their divorce, I had said something that caused them to argue. So, for many years, I believed I was the reason for "The Divorce."

I later learned that not all things are as they appear to be. Until a few years ago, I thought Alaska was by Hawaii and couldn't figure out why one got so hot and the other so cold. If you watch the news, they're right next to each other. And the map of the United States I had when I was little, with the plastic pieces that stick to the cardboard, also had them right next to each other.

In time, I realized I did not cause the divorce. And, one day, after watching the John Wayne movie "North to Alaska," again, I was singing the song. I was trying to figure out just how far south you had to be to go north to Alaska. Australia maybe? I decided to ask my husband (I think he's still laughing). By golly, I would have to go north to Alaska. It's by CANADA!! Oh, the deception.

And, yes, I remember exactly what I said that night. I will remember it until the day I die. I may not remember what I had for dinner last night (and I don't), but I'll remember this. I had asked my mom if I could have hoop earrings. Not the big hoops, just the little ones. What I didn't know, my parents had a "history" when it comes to hoop earrings. So, no, I didn't get the earrings. And the final straw; they sold our home. Divorce is devastating. I got over it, but it took a long time. A very long time.

From the Frying Pan into the Fire

After living with our mom for about a year, my sister and I moved in with our dad. He was dating a nice lady and one day both our families went to Marine World. While I was eating two blue cotton candies (the biggest cotton candies I have ever seen, and only 75 cents each!) we talked about them getting married, us moving into her home, and my sister and I changing high schools. My dad said to me, "You're really going from the frying pan into the fire." At the time, I didn't realize how true those words were.

They married, and I was now living in a world very foreign to me. I was part of a blended family. What they say is true. It's hard to make it work. Very hard. I was now one of five kids and one was a boy. I had a brother. That was really weird. The thing that bothered me the most was that I had always been "Daddy's Girl," and now there was a cute little 5-year-old girl calling *my* dad "Daddy." Not good, not good at all. I would share anything I had, or even give it away, but share my *daddy*? I don't think so. And now, since we were living in a different school district, I had to leave all my friends. I know I said I would; but it's one thing to talk about it, and another thing to actually do it.

Nothing was familiar anymore. I was very lonely and I didn't handle it well. I was also very naïve and painfully shy (I know, hard to believe now). In high school I was so shy I wouldn't even take my coat off before class. I was terrified I might make eye contact with someone while I was standing there, and it might be a boy. Oh the horror.

I now realize I didn't make life easy for my dad and step-mom, and I feel really bad about that. To think, she would make us bacon pancakes *before* school, and *before* she went to work! BACON pancakes, *who knew*? YUM! What an ungrateful child I was. Before "The Divorce" Debbie and I made breakfast every morning. EGGO waffles and coffee for our parents (the old-fashioned way—no Mr. Coffee). We would get them up when it was ready. What a difference. And that new little sister, yeah, she probably didn't like me calling her mommy, "mom" either. Hmmm. I *really* want a do-over. And the reason blended families are so hard to make work; kids like me.

"God On Call"

Unfortunately, it didn't take me long to find out a whole other world was open to me. My "new world" was giving me opportunities I didn't even know existed. They weren't all good ones either. I was like a kid in a candy store. And I love candy.

Now I just wanted to have fun. The kind of fun God does not approve of and parents aren't aware of...like smoking. And not just cigarettes. Some of it was peer pressure, but the decisions I made were still mine. And as we all know, when you're fifteen, you know *everything*. You really have no idea just how bad I want a do-over.

I no longer went to church. Big mistake. I didn't quit believing in God; I just didn't have room for Him in my life anymore. And since I didn't have an intimate relationship with Jesus, or even know what one was, He was the first in my life to go. Looking back, I guess I had an "I believe in God, I know there's a Heaven and a hell and I know I'm going to Heaven, and I pray when someone needs something" relationship with Him. I learned the hard way that going to church was more important than I realized. I still prayed, but only in emergencies. I guess that's when my "God on Call" relationship began.

My life was headed in a direction I hadn't planned on. Needless to say, my high school years weren't very productive. And since my dream of becoming a teacher had been derailed, I now had no reason to go to college. I did my best to get through high school as anonymously as possible, with the least amount of work. I managed to do a good job at both.

When you fail to plan, you plan to fail. *Now* I know. Since I didn't have any goals, I just continued to have fun. There would be time to get serious later.

I wish when I was younger someone, anyone, would have asked me what my favorite thing to do was, and then headed me in that direction for a career. I loved to read, and I loved books. Still do. Back then, they still had proofreaders. Reading for a living. Wouldn't that have been a cool job? Oh my gosh! Any job at a publishing company would have been awesome, or even a job in a library. I actually went to the Lodi Public Library to apply for a job. They said I needed a college degree. Refer to "Failure to Plan." Soooo, why didn't I go to night school then?!?! Obviously, not as smart a teenager as I thought I was. *Anyhoo*, let it go, Lori, just let it go.

After high school, I thought life was great. It really wasn't, but I didn't know that. I mean, it was okay, but I didn't have any direction. I always had a job, but not a career. I was always waiting, but I didn't know what for. I guess I was waiting for *better*. Like I said, I was having fun...still doing drugs. But eventually, the fun caught up with me. I didn't even realize it when my world started to get smaller and smaller. The places I went and the people I saw were limited. I wasn't living, only existing, and I didn't even know it. The day finally came when life wasn't fun anymore. It was just sad. Even as bad as it was, I know it could have been much worse, and I'm very blessed that it wasn't.

To this day, I'm so grateful that I don't like needles. It's so bad that after I get lab work done, I wouldn't be able to pick out my phlebotomist in a one-person lineup. I can't look at the person drawing my blood because I might see the needle, or the blood for that matter. I don't do blood. And, after trying a few kinds, I can honestly say that I don't like the taste of *any* alcohol. That includes beer and wine. I don't know why, but for some reason, I always get asked if I want a glass of wine or a beer when I say I don't drink. They all stink and they all taste like they smell. So, becoming an alcoholic wasn't gonna happen. Thank God, literally. I discovered I have an addictive personality; speed and cigarettes were bad enough.

I didn't want to live that life anymore, but I was not able to stop on my own. Fortunately, I remembered I had "God on Call." And, of course, He was right there where I had left Him, patiently waiting for me to come back to Him. I began to pray every day asking God to deliver me. And He did. Nowhere in the Bible does Jesus say, "I'm going back to Heaven now. You're on your own." No, quite the opposite, actually. He said, "…I will never leave you nor forsake you." Believe me, if I can quit doing drugs, anyone can. But I couldn't do it without God. If you're praying for someone, don't stop. My grandmas prayed for me from the day I was born till the days they died. Through the good times and the heart-wrenching sad times in my life their love and prayers for me never wavered. They didn't know specifics. They didn't have to. God knew. They just prayed. Because they loved me. And God did the rest.

The worst part is, God knows everything. It breaks my heart when I break His heart.

There is a section in my Bible called, "What the Bible Says About Grieving the Holy Spirit." In Ephesians chapter 4, verse 30, the Apostle Paul says, "Do not grieve the Holy Spirit of God." We grieve Him when we disobey God's commandments, when we know what to do and then choose to do the opposite. Basically, what Paul said was, "Your ungodly behavior breaks the heart of God." It feels like he's talking directly to me, and that makes me wanna cry. Fortunately, I know He is a loving and forgiving God. But still….

I was now drug free. And after the way I had been living, I figured I was pretty blessed just to be alive. I should have been in jail, or dead. Both, actually. It was only by the grace of God I never overdosed or went to jail. I thanked God for delivering me from the depths of hell and took control of my life back. Because that had gone so well for me in the past. Yep. I so quickly and easily forgot *why* things got better. God answered my prayers and I basically said, "Thanks, see ya." He must love me an awful lot.

"Take It"

Several years ago, I accidentally went back to work in escrow. I say "accidentally," because I had worked in escrow twice before, and both times had said "never again." Here's a tip: *Never* say never. For when you do, you have just made certain it's going to happen. I don't know why that is. I'm not superstitious, but it always seems to happen. Oh wait, it just dawned on me…that just could be God showing us who *really* is in control. Huh, *could* be.

Looking back, my third return to escrow was obviously *God's* awesome plan for my life because it certainly wasn't mine. I loved the work I did as an escrow officer, but the stress was killing me. When it got to the point where I just wanted to get through the day without having chest pains and headaches, I knew I had to do something. My stomach was always in a knot, and I worried about the job 24/7. It's called "escrow hell."

Came the day when I just wanted it to stop. I didn't want to be there. I didn't want to answer the phone. I didn't want to draw anymore escrow instructions. I never wanted to see another loan package. I just wanted to sit down and cry.

Watching "In Touch" with Dr. Charles Stanley I knew God cared about every area of my life. I also knew He wanted me to surrender my all to Him...but not my job, right? I wanted God in my life in *most* places, to help, but not to control. No one can do that better than I can. It's hard to let go of control. Very hard. And yes, He did want me to surrender my job to Him. And deep down I knew it. I just had to figure out how I was going to surrender my job to Him and still retain control. I think I kinda wanted Him to fix it and then get out of my way again. What's wrong with me? And yet, God still did not turn and run as fast as He could from me. Although, He should have.

Knowing God wants me to surrender my all to Him and actually doing it are two totally different things. Kinda like changing high schools: "You want me to do *what*?" I couldn't seem to get past that "on call" relationship I had going with Him. I was watching "In Touch" on Sundays, tithing, praying when I, or someone I knew, needed prayer, and trying very hard to be a good person. "But...but...but...I'm an escrow officer. I *have* to be in control." This was a *huge* struggle for me. Growing up, all I ever heard in church was hellfire and brimstone. I never heard the words "intimate relationship with God" until I started listening to Dr. Stanley. I knew I wanted, and needed, that in my life *NOW. And I was going to start by relinquishing control of my job???* Yeah, that'll work.

But I had to do something. I figured it was worth a try...even if I was sure it wouldn't work. I said, "God, I can't do it anymore. Help me." And very much to my surprise, it was that easy. Immediately, the Holy Spirit reminded me of Bible verse Matthew 11:28, "Come to Me, all you who labor and are heavy laden, and I will give you rest." Rest. To rest in God's arms. Yeah, I wanted that. I wanted that more than anything.

I knew God was worthy of me getting on my knees before Him when I prayed, but I used my job as an excuse not to get out of bed even ten minutes early to pray. Since I wouldn't make time for God, I would have to start with something quick and easy. I decided to start with the easiest thing I could think of: praying in the shower. It wouldn't take any time out of my day, and I was multi-tasking. Good girl. Very smart.

As I was getting in the shower each morning I would say, "Good morning, God," and then I would say, "This is the day the Lord has made; I will rejoice and be glad in it." I didn't realize it was a Bible verse, Psalm 118:24, until I read it in my Bible a few years later. I just thought it was a good way to start my day.

I remembered learning Matthew 6:8-13 where Jesus tells us, "For your Father knows the things you have need of before you ask Him. In this manner, therefore, pray: Our Father who art in Heaven, hallowed be Thy Name, Thy kingdom come, Thy will be done, on earth as it is in Heaven. Give us this day our daily bread and forgive us our trespasses as we forgive those who trespass against us. Lead us not into temptation, but deliver us from evil. For Thine is the kingdom, the power and the glory forever, Amen." After saying that prayer, also known as The Lord's Prayer, I would praise God. I would thank Him for giving me a job so close to home (I worked a mile from our house). I thanked Him that every day was one less day I would have to do the job. I thanked Him for healthy families, for my wonderful husband, Gary, and that we are so loved. It felt good. And remember, this didn't interfere with my day. I prayed all this in the shower.

On the way to work, I would ask Him to "Take it," because I couldn't carry the burden anymore. I needed *Him* to carry the load. I would say, "God, I give my job to You. You are in total control. Just let me know what to do, when to do it, and how to do it."

I started saying Bible verses to remind myself that God doesn't want me to worry about anything. It also helped keep my focus on God, not my situation.

I wanted things from God, but not material things. I wanted His perfect peace, joy and contentment. I wanted Him to take away all my problems, worries, fears, anxieties and stress. I wanted Him to take it all. In escrow, there are plenty of things to stress over and worry about. Like getting the escrow instructions and funding packages done correctly and on time, putting recording documents on hold, releasing a hold, getting the closings done and the checks out on time, taking phone calls all day and still trying to get the work done. I can't tell you how many times I woke up in the middle of the night, trying to remember if I put a hold, or released a hold, on recording documents. And, my personal favorite, getting a rush escrow that wants to close in three days, stopping everything else I'm doing, getting it done on time, and then they decide they don't want to close escrow for several more months. Or it cancels altogether. Sure, no problem.

Philippians 4:13 is a verse I started reciting about every ten minutes. "I can do all things through Christ who strengthens me." I started saying this one to remind myself I wasn't doing my job in my strength, but in God's strength. What a relief!! When I know everything is possible *with* God, why would I ever want to do anything *without* Him? Oh, I wouldn't.

During my workday, when things would start piling up, I would say, "God, take it, You're in control." Almost immediately, people would call and reschedule appointments. And things I had to do wouldn't take nearly as long as they normally would. He was doing what He said He would, taking my burdens and giving me rest. He was answering my prayers by de-stressing my life at work. What probably surprised me the most was how quickly God worked. I would barely get the words "Help me" out of my mouth and help was there. Once I saw what a great job God was doing, way better than I ever did, I wanted Him to have total control. I tell you, watching a faithful God at work in my life was, and is, an amazing experience. God can do anything. There is *nothing* He will not do to help me if I ask, and then get out of His way. After seeing what God had already done, and so quickly, I wanted more God, much more. I had fought for so long to retain control of my job, but now I didn't want any part of control. It felt so good to breathe.

Every week, at the end of his church service, Charles Stanley would say, "Obey God and leave all the consequences to Him." Putting these words into action is how I learned to be obedient. I constantly reminded myself to obey God and leave all the consequences to Him. I did this by giving control to God and leaving the outcome to Him. Then I would remind God that when I'm obedient, He's gonna have to do the rest because His word is His promise. You see, God didn't want me to stress over my job. He didn't want me to fight Him for control of it either. He wanted me to rest in His loving arms. And I wanted to...very much. (Matthew 11:28 again.)

When things got stressful and I would obey God by giving my problem to Him (usually too much work and too little time), that meant I couldn't worry anymore. No matter what happened, I had to trust that God was in control, and everything would work out. I had to leave the consequences to Him. I never knew how it would work out; I just knew it would. And it did. Every time. God has never, ever, ever failed me, and He never, ever, ever will; because it is impossible for Him to do so.

It didn't happen overnight, but it didn't take long for me to remember to give Him my problem as soon as I got one. Every once in a while, I'd catch myself worrying about something and then I would remember, "Obey God and leave all the consequences to Him." This was, and still is, my favorite saying. It also helped me in knowing what to do in any given situation. I would remind myself to "Do what's right and everything else will follow." I always knew the right thing to do; it's just not always the easiest. But it's the one that enables me to sleep at night. When I do what's right I know I'm obeying God, then everything else that follows is in His hands, not mine.

I also learned that, through God, I have the ability to bind Satan. This is very important. I know

Satan can only be in one place at a time, but it sure feels like the closer I get to God, the more Satan attacks me. So, when I notice signs of Satan creeping in, I say "Satan, right this second, I bind you and command you to flee in the name of Jesus Christ, my Lord and Savior. And you must flee now." Then I thank Jesus for giving me power and authority over Satan, and for reminding me to use it. Sometimes I'll quote a scripture or two. Satan really hates that. I am confident doing this, as I have all of God's power available to me through the Holy Spirit who lives in me. Knowing that I have the power of God in me, no matter what I'm doing, is, well, awesome.

I also kept three sayings in mind to help me remember to live a godly life:

1. **"Only what's done for Christ will last":**
1 Corinthians 3:12-15, "…each one's work will become clear…because it will be revealed by fire; and the fire will test each one's work…if anyone's work which he has built on it endures, he will receive a reward…."

2. **"When you do for the least of these, you do for Me":**
Matthew 25:34-46, "…Come, you blessed of My Father, inherit the kingdom prepared for you…for I was hungry and you gave Me food…. Then the righteous will answer Him saying, Lord when did we see You hungry and feed You…. And the King will answer and say to them, Assuredly, I say to you,

inasmuch as you did it to one of the least of these, My brethren, you did it to Me…"

3. **"Do not let your left hand know what your right hand is doing":**
Matthew 6:3-4, "But when you do a charitable deed, do not let your left hand know what your right hand is doing, that your charitable deed may be in secret; and your Father who sees in secret will Himself reward you openly."

Obey God and leave all the consequences to Him. (Repeat as needed until it becomes a way of life.)

Blessings of Obedience

On the weekends, I started saying my prayers on my knees, for He is worthy. I began to see more blessings. Better yet, I started to feel closer to God and my prayer time increased. Sometimes I would even stay long enough to listen. I noticed that when I listened, I actually heard from God. My talking time decreased, and my listening time greatly increased. Now, sometimes all I say is, "I'm listening." And all I do is listen…and learn. There's something so peaceful and comforting about spending time alone with God.

When I returned to work my husband, Gary, and I decided I would work for five years. Less than four years later, Gary told me he wanted me to quit my job. He wanted me home when he's home because he's gone a lot and he missed me. Well, that was one of the best days of my life. His job had changed, and we were now in a position for me not to have to work.

This new life and closer walk with God was starting out really well. My walk with God wasn't even a year old yet, and the only life-changes I made were praying and letting go.

I had no idea God would bless me in so many ways I didn't even know were possible. Who knew quitting my job so soon was even an option? Oh yeah, God did. Personally, I never thought I was going to be able to quit, even after five years. I figured if I didn't die of a heart attack, I would just keel over at my desk when I was eighty-something. I didn't have much of a future to look forward to. But *now*! More, please.

I didn't start praying so I could quit my job. I started praying because I wanted a better life. I didn't know how God was going to make that happen, I just knew He could and had faith that He would.

One day I told Gary, because of my obedience, God blessed me with not having to work. Gary responded with, it's because of the job God blessed me with, that you're able to stay home. Potato/potado. I'm still retired. He's still working.

Now to my home life. I used to worry about *everything*. And the "what ifs." Oh my gosh, every day had another "what if." I was making myself crazy. And to top it off, I was now a caregiver for one of our parents as well. So now I not only had to worry about everything in our lives, but I had to worry about her as well. The faster I ran, the behind-er I got.

It took me awhile, but I finally realized I could have the same outcome with my home life that I had with my job. Yeah, you would think I would have figured that out, say, *sooner*. I took my favorite saying and started applying it at home. "Obey God and leave all the consequences to Him." The same things I had been doing at work I started doing at home. Who knew?? Oh, yeah, God did.

I started to give God my daily schedule, because it never went the way I thought it would go anyway. I needed to obey God by giving Him control of my day and leave the consequences to Him. So when my already booked-solid day got more hectic, I had to let go. The same things that used to happen at work would happen in my home life. Appointments would cancel. Parents would change their mind about wanting something. My day would become manageable. I watched, in awe, as God worked in my life. And you know what I came to realize? Not one "what if" ever happened.

During this time, Gary was away at work fifty percent of the time, so I was in control of everything: our home, yard, bills, parents, etc. I wanted everything to be perfect so he wouldn't have a care in the world when he was at home. So, when something broke or needed replacing, like the water heater, the air conditioner, the washer, etc., I handled it by putting God in control. I would say, "God, enable me to know what to do here." And He would. Made my life real easy.

One day Gary pointed out that God does not want me to play the lottery. Will miracles never cease?? I was a faithful lottery player. My plan was to win and get a different car. Gary had been trying to get me to buy one for more than two years because he loves to spoil me, but I didn't want to spend the money. I knew he was right about the lottery though, so I quit playing. As soon as I quit, I got that warm fuzzy feeling I get when I'm in God's will. Gary started talking about the car again, and instead of giving him reasons why we shouldn't get the car, I started looking for one. Exactly one week later, there it was, the car Gary had been talking about, same color and all. I named it God's Gift, because that's what it was. Every time I look at the car, I'm reminded of how God blesses obedience; and I'm still thanking Him for it 14 years later. I don't take any blessings for granted and I haven't played the lottery since. Ok, maybe once. And that's four dollars I'll never get back.

The things I did then are the same things I'm doing now. Like when life starts to get a little hectic, I tell God what I'm planning on doing, but ask Him to show me what *He* wants me to do. It never fails... my commitments and appointments are either cancelled or rescheduled so that everything works out in perfect timing. And giving God control, daily, of every area of my life, including my marriage, just takes the load off.

What never ceases to amaze me is the abundance of blessings God pours out on me. It's nothing to receive several a day. I frequently hear myself say, "Wow, I didn't even know that was possible." Some things seem impossible to me; other things I know are possible, but I'd never expected them to happen to me in a million years.

I also ask God to open my eyes so I will be able to see all the blessings He has for me. I know that every day God blesses me in ways I'm not even aware of. I want to be able to thank Him for those as well.

Remember, only what's done for Christ will last. And when we do for the least of these, we do for Him. When you open the door for someone who is having trouble walking, or who is in a wheelchair, you are doing it for Christ. When you give $20 to a family living out of their car, you are doing it for Christ. These are the things that matter, the things done for Christ, the things that last. When you do for others, it comes back to you, more, and better. Material things burn in a fire. Kindness doesn't. Remember, "fire will test each one's work." And, yes, God does want us to have material things. He just doesn't want us to make anyone or anything else our idols.

A good example of obedience in the Bible is Noah, the flood guy. In the first Book of the Bible, Genesis, God saw that all men had become wicked and every thought of theirs was evil, continually, and He was grieved in His heart. So, the Lord said, "I will destroy man whom I have created from the face of the earth, both man and beast, creeping things and birds of the air, for I am sorry that I have made them," Genesis 6:7. ALL of them, except for one man and his family. Noah. WOW!! Only *one* good man and his family?? That's not good. This is, like, six pages into the Bible and man is already so evil that God is sorry he made them. Boy, that one bite of apple Adam and Eve each took really made a mess of things!

Noah was a just man who found grace in the eyes of God. God told Noah that He was going to bring floodwaters on the earth to destroy it. He proceeded to tell Noah that He wanted him to build an ark, and exactly how He wanted the ark to be built. The measurements, what kind of wood, how many rooms, etc. God also told him that two of every animal and bird would be coming to the ark. Catch that one? The animals will be *coming* to the ark. Noah didn't have to go get them. Meaning, God is in control of the animals as well. Huh. Pretty cool. He even told Noah how much food he was to take.

Up until this point in the Bible, there has never been any mention of rain. Genesis 2:6 says, "...but a mist went up from the earth and watered the whole face of the ground." So, it's quite possible that Noah had never seen rain. Definitely not a flood. Either way, what *faith* it took to be so obedient. Thankfully he was, because Noah, his wife, their three sons and their wives were the only living humans after the flood. Genesis 9:1, "So God blessed Noah and his sons, and said to them: 'Be fruitful and multiply, and fill the earth.'"

I can't even imagine what must have been going through his mind when God was telling him all these things. Flood, ark, only living humans. Yet, Noah did everything God asked of him. How frightening the unknown must have been. But, when you walk with God, like Noah did, you know that faithfulness is always rewarded, and you never have to fear...anything.

Fun Fact: This is also when the first rainbow appears. God made a covenant with Noah, his descendants and every living thing, that He would never again destroy every living thing by flood. God said He was going to set His rainbow in the cloud and every time He brings a cloud over the earth the rainbow will be seen, and He will remember His covenant.

That is just one story. There is story after story like this in the Bible. When the people were obedient, God blessed them. When they turned their back on Him, there were consequences.

Even though I was watching a church service on television, Gary informed me that God wanted me to *go* to church as well. How did he know that? He was right. But how did he know that?? Hmmm.

Another act of obedience on my part was no more work on Sundays. That is my Sabbath, and in the Bible, God told us not to work on the Sabbath. I cook, but that's it. Try it. I promise you will get more done in six days than you ever did in seven. Why? Because obedience always brings blessings and blesses our loved ones as well. Also, taking a day to rest rejuvenates you. The first Sunday is hard, because you can't imagine losing a day of work. But you'll see. When you're obedient, God is faithful. If it can't be Sunday, choose another day. When you think about it, pastors work on Sundays. And for some people, like one of my grandmas, her day of rest was Saturday. The Bible says that God worked for six days creating the heavens and the earth and all that is in them, and on the seventh day He rested. Since God doesn't get tired, that was His example to us of how *we* are supposed to live.

When I found myself with a few extra minutes, I changed how I spent them. Here are a few examples of what I did that you can do as well:

Turn off the radio in the car and thank God you have a healthy family (2 seconds).

Stop by and see your mom and/or dad, or a loved one, just because you can (5 minutes, usually; it's longer with some moms).

Call your spouse and say, "This is just an "I love you" call. Talk to you later" (3 seconds).

When you get up in the morning, kneel down and say, "Good morning, God" (1 second).

Before you get into bed, kneel down and say, "Thank you, God" (1 second).

Mute the commercial and just listen to God (3 minutes).

Read your Bible, Genesis 1:1, the first paragraph of the Bible (3 seconds).

Say Bible verses in the shower (no time out of your day...you're multi-tasking).

Say Bible verses in the car (no time out of your day...you're multi-tasking).

These are small things. But they are mighty. They were the beginnings of what changed my life, completely. Now I rarely turn my radio on in the car. It's a perfect God and me time.

I still repeat James 1:17 several times a day, "Every good gift and every perfect gift is from above." Saying this reminds me that I am continually receiving God's best. And any better is impossible.

God wants us to be in position to receive His maximum blessings at all times. When we're not being blessed, it's not God's fault, it's ours.

Obey God and leave all the consequences to Him.

Overcoming Addiction

Now that I was no longer in escrow my reason, uh, excuse, for still smoking was gone. For years I knew I *should* quit smoking, main reason being, God didn't want me to smoke. Another being my health. One day I asked Gary if he would kiss me more if I quit smoking. He said, "I'll kiss you longer, because you'll live longer." I now went from 'should quit' to 'really, really, really want to quit.' I tried several times and failed miserably. Finally, I asked God to help me. You know…when all else fails. He prompted me to read Life Principle No. 8 in my Life Principles Bible: Fight all your battles on your knees and you win every time.

I gave my addiction to God, and two days later I quit. I thought I was going to need Nicorette gum to help me quit, but I didn't want to get addicted to that as well. I asked God to prevent me from becoming addicted to it, and He answered my prayer. I used three pieces of gum in the two days it took me to quit smoking and I've never used it since.

Whenever I had the urge to smoke, I asked God to take it away and He would. I had to ask Him to do this about every 20 minutes at first; but then the urges got further and further apart. It wasn't long before all thought and desire was gone. I had smoked for 32 years, and I would have bet one million dollars I would not be able to quit for even one day. But once I let go and put God in control, He was right there helping me every time I called on Him. I fought this battle on my knees. And I won! It ended up being one of the easiest things I have ever done. Quitting smoking. One of the easiest things I have ever done. Doesn't even sound right, but it's true. Philippians 4:13 again, "I can do all things through Christ who strengthens me." It doesn't say, "I can do all things on my own because I'm an amazing person."

On June 16, 2010, the third anniversary of the day I never thought would be possible, I received a beautiful bouquet of flowers from my husband. And the card said: "I'll love you longer."

Obey God and leave all the consequences to Him.

Life Principles

Since Life Principle No. 8 worked so well, I decided to read all 30 of them. Fortunately, it finally sunk in that they are all meant for me as well. Here's a couple more:

Life Principle No. 27: *Prayer is life's greatest time saver.*

Saying my morning prayers on my knees has been life changing. I still pray anywhere and everywhere, but it's not quite the same as praying on my knees. Kneeling in "our place," shoes off, may not be Holy Ground, but I feel His presence. It never fails, when I start my day in prayer, the day always goes better. Everything gets done. Not always, in fact, rarely, the things *I* thought needed to be done, but everything *God* wanted done. And in perfect timing.

Life Principle No. 26: *Adversity is a bridge to a deeper relationship with God.*

Working as an escrow officer was the adversity that led to my deeper relationship with God. Once I gave control to God, the pressure was off me and on Him to do a good job. And since I know God doesn't stress about anything, we were good to go. I was finally okay with being back in escrow for as long as God wanted me there. Funny, once I was okay with it, He got me out.

Obey God and leave all the consequences to Him.

God's Word—Our Instruction Book

"Your word is a lamp to my feet and a light to

my path," Psalm 119:105.

Let's say you buy a new product, and you don't know how it works. You would read the instruction manual, wouldn't you? Ok. Not if you're a man, but let's make an exception here. The Bible is our instruction manual. In it, God not only tells us everything we need to know about Him and *His* ways, but also how *we* are supposed to live.

To know how God is working in my life, I have to know His ways. To know the ways of God, I have to read the Bible. When I read the Bible, I learn His ways. I see the way He answers prayer. How He makes a shepherd boy into a king. How He blesses obedience and hands down consequences for disobedience. The way He guides, protects, feeds and clothes. The way He saves and destroys. And the way He shows mercy and gives grace. These are just a few of the ways of God.

By reading the Bible, I learned what to do to be the most blessed, and what not to do to prevent God's wrath. I learned how to have perfect peace in every situation...give it to God. I learned what it takes to have an intimate relationship with God. I had always loved God, but I had never made the effort to get to know Him. Now, if I could just apply the lessons I learned a little more often. God and I would *both* like that

The first book of the Bible is called Genesis, meaning "first." This book tells how the earth was made and the beginning of mankind, the beginning of everything actually. Here's a hint: "In the beginning God created the heavens and the earth,"

Chapter 1, verse 1.

Somewhere I read that sharks have been around longer than trees. Since everything can be found in the Bible, I checked to see if this is true. On this, I'm going to have to *respectfully* agree to disagree with those who believe this. Genesis 1:11, Then God said, "Let the earth bring forth grass...the fruit tree...." Not until verse 20 did God say, "Let the waters abound with an abundance of living creatures and let birds fly above the earth...." So, I'm going with that.

The second book is called Exodus, meaning "a mass departure of people." And that's exactly what happens in this book. God sent Moses to lead the enslaved Israelites out of Egypt and to the Promised Land. When they got to the Red Sea, God parted it so they could walk across on dry land. When the Egyptian army, who was chasing them, got there, God released the water, and the entire army was drowned. God not only provided their protection along the way, but also their food, water, healing, etc. God did everything. And that's exactly what I ask Him to do for me—everything.

The Book of Proverbs basically tells us how we can live a godly life in an ungodly world. It was mostly written by Solomon. He was the wisest king that ever lived.

Proverbs 16:16 says, "How much better to get wisdom than gold! And to get understanding is to be chosen rather than silver." Wow! Wisdom, understanding, must be pretty important. Proverbs also tells us how to deal with everyday life relating to God, parents, children, neighbors, government, etc.

Fun Fact: You've heard the saying, "Pride goes before the fall." Yep, that's in there, Proverbs 16:18. And you know the other saying that I've used, "If you want to make God laugh, tell Him your plans." Looks like it just might have come from Proverbs 16:9, "A man's heart plans his way. But the Lord directs his steps." I'm starting to think the Bible is quoted by a lot of people who don't even know they're quoting the Bible. And sometimes…it's me.

In The Book of Daniel there are three young men, Shadrach, Meshach and Abed-Nego, who loved God and would not serve other gods or bow down and worship a gold image (an idol) that King Nebuchadnezzar commanded everyone do. They were bound and thrown into a fiery furnace. The fire was so hot it killed the men who threw them into the fire. When the king looked, he saw four men, loose and walking in the midst of the fire, unhurt. Then the king said, "…the fourth is like the Son of God." When they came out of the fire, not one hair on their head was singed and they did not smell like smoke. The best part about this: it made a believer out of the king. He said, "Blessed be the God of Shadrach, Meshach and Abed-Nego…." He also said God delivered them because of their trust in Him and no other God can deliver like this. WOW!!

It went the same way with Daniel. He was thrown into the lions' den for praying to God, instead of the king; but no harm came to him because God kept the lions' mouths shut. When the king saw that he was alive, he rejoiced because he liked Daniel and knew that he had been set up. So, the king had Daniel's accusers and their families thrown into the same lions' den. The lions overpowered them and broke all their bones to pieces before they ever got to the bottom of the den.

Then King Darius said that Daniel's God is the living God who delivers and rescues, like He rescued Daniel from the power of the lions.

I learned that when we obey God, He not only blesses our obedience, but He also goes through our trials with us. He will never leave us or forsake us. Ever. And whether we know it or not, people are watching us to see how we live. Just like they were watching Daniel and the three young men.

The last book of the Bible, Revelation, tells us how it's all going to end. And it's not pretty. But I'm not worried. I'm not going to be here when it happens. If I haven't already passed away at a ripe old age, I'm going to meet Jesus in the sky when He returns for His saints...like me.

This instruction manual even comes with a support line. Prayer is our direct phone line to God. And we can call Him anytime, day or night, 24/7/365. When we have questions, we have access to the actual Creator, the One who wrote the manual. The phone line works both ways. When the Holy Spirit is prompting us for whatever reason, that is God calling us. Prayer is us calling God. So, when you need help or just have a question, like

Andy said, "Aunt Bee, call the man."

There is no wrong place to start reading the Bible. It's just important that we read it. To this day, before I start reading, I always ask God to give me wisdom, knowledge and understanding. And He does. (Because I remember they are better to have than gold or silver.)

Once I remembered that the promises God made to the people in the Bible were for us as well, I started reading the Bible as if God was talking to me personally. I found a verse I continue to say daily, Genesis 15:1. It says, "…Do not be afraid, I am your shield, your exceedingly great reward." This verse reminds me I have nothing to fear, because God is protecting me at all times. And as long as my focus is on Him, I am rewarded in ways I couldn't come up with in a million years—my greatest reward being my relationship with Him.

Many times throughout the Bible, Jesus says, "Fear not." "Be not afraid." "Do not fear." "Peace I leave with you." "I came to bring peace." "In Me you have peace." I knew these words were meant for me as well. So before long, all my fears were gone, and His perfect peace had taken their place.

The more I read, the more I learned about the character of God and His promises. It all became clear. Anything you want to know is answered somewhere in the Bible.

I believe the Bible is "God-breathed." And if I believe one verse, I have to believe them all. And I do. "The entirety of Your word is truth," Psalm 119:160.

Obey God and leave all the consequences to Him.

The Ways of God

The following stories are good examples of the ways of God:

David

Some of the Bible guys are known for more than one thing. Like David. He is the guy in David and Goliath, David and Bathsheba and the shepherd boy who became a king.

When people looked at David, they saw a shepherd boy. When God looked at David, He saw a king. David had a heart bent toward God. Because David was obedient, God used him to do great and mighty things. Who, but God, would send a boy, armed only with a sling and five smooth stones, to kill a 9-foot-tall soldier decked out in full armor? By the way, David had four stones more than he needed.

In 2 Samuel 22:20-22, David talks about how God delivered him from his enemies. He says, in part, "He delivered me because He delighted in me. The Lord rewarded me according to my righteousness; …For I have kept the ways of the Lord." David was obedient, and richly rewarded because of it.

In 2 Samuel 12:7-8, God said to King David, "I anointed you king over Israel, and I delivered you from the hand of Saul. I gave you your master's house and your master's wives into your keeping, and gave you the house of Israel and Judah. And if that had been too little, I also would have given you much more!"

What more? God had blessed David with everything, so it seems. Yet, God still had more to give. God's abundance is endless. He owns it all.

Solomon

God told David that when he died his son Solomon would become king. So before he died, David instructed Solomon to keep the ways of the Lord. Solomon loved the Lord, and one night the Lord appeared to Solomon in a dream and said, "Ask! What shall I give you?" Solomon was still a child and did not know how to rule; so he asked God to give him an understanding heart to judge God's people, and discernment between good and evil. God told Solomon, that because he had not asked for long life or riches, He would give him a wise and understanding heart, so that there has not been anyone like him before or after.

Then God said to Solomon, "And I have also given you what you have not asked: both riches and honor, so that there shall not be anyone like you among the kings all your days. So, if you walk in My ways, to keep my statues and My commandments, as your father David walked, then I will lengthen your days." Huh, God can even lengthen our days. Wow. Solomon was the wisest, richest king that ever lived. This is the guy that wrote most of The Book of Proverbs.

Job

When you hear it said that someone has "the patience of Job," he's the one. God considered Job to be a blameless and upright man; one who feared Him and shunned evil. So, of course, Satan wanted to destroy him. One day, Satan told God that Job was only that way because He protected him, and if He took away the protection, Job would curse Him to His face. So, the Lord said to Satan, "Behold, all that he has is in your power; only do not lay a hand on his person." Hang on a second. God and Satan...*talk*? Huh. *Who knew*?

Everything Job had Satan took from him. Seven sons, three daughters, 7,000 sheep, 3,000 camels, 500 yoke of oxen, 500 female donkeys, and a very large household. All of his children and servants were killed, and his animals were either stolen or killed. He still did not curse God. So, Satan told God that Job would curse Him if his health was afflicted. God told Satan he could attack Job, but he must spare his life. Satan struck Job with painful boils from the sole of his foot to the crown of his head. Job still would not curse God. But Satan was showing *his* true colors...pure evil.

Because Job was so patient and obedient, after a time God restored everything that Satan had taken from him. But God didn't just give Job what was taken from him; He gave Job *twice* as much as he had before, along with his seven sons and three daughters. And the daughters were the most beautiful women in all the land. Then, Job lived a hundred and forty *more* years. Fun Fact: The Job's

Daughters organization is named after Job's daughters.

The Israelites and the Promised Land

Now, one would think that God's chosen people, the Israelites, would be the most obedient, faithful, trusting, grateful people in all the land. Well, one would be wrong—very wrong. Instead of praising and thanking God for delivering them out of 400 years of slavery, and providing ALL their needs, they repeatedly turned their backs on God and worshipped idols. God's *chosen* people. Worshipping idols. Huh.

In Exodus 3:8 God says, "So I have come down to deliver them out of the hand of the Egyptians, and to bring them up from that land to a good and large land, to a land flowing with milk and honey, to the place of the Canaanites...." And that's exactly what He did, and in a relatively short amount of time.

The Book of Numbers, chapters 13 and 14, tell the story. When they got there the Lord spoke to Moses, saying, "Send men to spy out the land of Canaan, which I am giving to the children of Israel...." (They are already there and haven't done their 40 years in the wilderness yet.)

Before going into the Promised Land, Moses obeyed God and sent the twelve men. They spied out the Promised Land for 40 days. They all reported back that the land indeed is flowing with milk and honey, just like God had said. They even brought back one bunch of grapes that was so big it had to be carried on a pole between two men. But ten of them said the cities are fortified, the people are strong, some like giants, and the land devours its inhabitants. Therefore, their bad report scared the Israelites, and they would not go in. But the other two, Caleb and Joshua, reminded the people that God is with them, and going before them to fight their battles; making them well able to take the land. Just like He has done since they left Egypt. But the people turned on them and refused God's instruction to take possession of the land that He had given to them, the Promised Land. Big mistake. When God tells us to do something, He will do His part in making sure it happens, and we need to do ours.

When God heard this He was furious, telling Moses, because of their disobedience they will now roam the wilderness for 40 years, one year for each day the men were spying out the Promised Land. God also said that everyone 20 years old and above will perish in the wilderness. At the end of the 40 years, God allowed their *children* to enter in along with Caleb and Joshua, the two men who had said they should enter forty years previously. So, their consequence for disobedience was the 40 years in the wilderness along with not being allowed to go into the Promised Land, *at all*. *And* literally *dying* in the wilderness. That is some consequence. We never know just how much we lose by not obeying God.

Sometimes our trials seem like giants. Fear not, God is a giant slayer.

You know, God doesn't love us any less than He does David, Solomon or Job. So, every day I ask God for a heart bent toward Him like David's, for the wisdom of Solomon, the patience of Job, and to be as pleasing in His sight as Mary, the mother of Jesus. Just imagine how much Mary must have pleased God for Him to choose her to bear His Son. I want to make God that happy. And every day, I try.

Obey God and leave all the consequences to Him.

Drawing Near to God

James 4:8 says, "Draw near to God and He will draw near to you."

God has given me a free will. I wish He hadn't, but He did. So, it is my choice to get close to Him or live apart from Him. I want to be so close to God that you can't tell us apart. I want Him to be my first thought in the morning, utmost in my thoughts all day, and my last thought as I fall asleep at night. When people look at me, I want them to see Christ in me. When I talk, I want them to hear Him.

When I started reading the Bible again, I'd run across verses I wanted to remember. So, I started learning them. I would leave my Bible open on the kitchen counter while I did housework and memorize the verses. And instead of listening to music in the car I started praying and reciting Bible verses. It is very calming. Also, it's hard to get road rage when you're saying Bible verses.

The more God I put in my life, the more Christ-like I am. It doesn't take long of no God coming into my life to not see or hear much God coming out of me. You know the saying, "garbage in, garbage out." Yeah, it's like that.

When I started my walk with God, I used to pray for things like:

"If I could just win the lottery..."

"If you would just change my husband..."

"If I just had this, if you could just fix that..."

You get the picture. "Nothing wrong with me, it's my situation."

But as I drew nearer to God, I learned it wasn't my situation that needed changing. It was me. *WHAT*??!! I couldn't imagine what could *possibly* be wrong with me. But I started asking God to change me and bring to my attention things I needed to repent of and lay before Him. Needless to say, I was real busy, real fast. I asked Him to make me more Christlike, and for the fruit of His Spirit to be seen in me. I prayed for Him to make me into the person He has drawn me to be. Jeremiah 31:3 says, "... 'Yes, I have loved you with an everlasting love; therefore, with lovingkindness I have drawn you.'" To this day, every morning in my prayers I ask Him to make me into the person He has drawn me to be. Because every day is another opportunity to live the life He has planned for me.

Like the Bible says in Matthew 6:21, "For where your treasure is, there your heart will be also." I wanted to make God, and time with God, my treasure. So, every waking moment I made a conscious effort to keep my focus on God. FYI—there are A LOT of distractions in this world. But, before I knew it, the things I wanted in life changed. Things became less and less important and time with Him became priceless. The things I used to think were so important just didn't matter anymore. The only thing I really wanted was to be the person God wanted me to be, and to do His will in every area of my life. I used to think money made you rich. Now I know that I know that I know I'm the richest girl in the world because I have peace, joy and contentment. Money can't buy that. God gave them to me for free.

Obey God and leave all the consequences to Him.

Living in the Center of God's Will

Jeremiah 29:11-13 says, "'For I know the thoughts that I think toward you,' says the Lord, 'thoughts of peace and not of evil. To give you a future and a hope. Then you will call upon Me and go and pray to Me, and I will listen to you. And you will seek Me and find Me, when you search for Me with all your heart.'" I love those verses. The Lord has only good things planned for my life. When I talk to Him, He listens; when I look to Him, He's there; and when I listen, I hear Him.

For instance, God told me to write this book. He also instilled in me a love for writing and a desire to glorify Him. For about a year I had been feeling I was supposed to write something, but no topic ever felt right.

Ever since I got my relationship with Jesus, my friends had started asking me why I was happy and smiling all the time. All I could say was, "God."

One day I was visiting one of them and she asked me again. Once again, I told her, "God." I didn't know how else to explain it.

As I was driving home I heard God say, "Write that." I said, "Write what?" He said, "Write how you got to be smiling and happy all the time." So, I'm writing everything God tells me to, and now you're reading it. We thank you!

When I wanted to start living my life in the center of God's will, I had no idea how to do that. Turns out it's one of the easiest things in the world to find out. Ask Him. Yep, just ask Him. It's that easy. And I learned that by reading the Bible verses at the beginning of this section. I'm to pray to Him and He will listen. I'm to seek Him and I will find Him.

Every morning I make myself available to do the will of God by asking Him to show me His will for my life and to enable and equip me to do it in His timing and in His strength.

Whenever a new situation arises, I ask Him to make His will a "no-brainer" for me. When I believe God has told me what to do, I head in that direction. I either get an uneasy feeling about my decision, or a warm fuzzy feeling (like my heart is swelling up).

Either way, I don't worry because He knows I'm seeking His will. When I get off track, He puts me back on. When I miss an opportunity, He gives me another one. Actually, He gives me as many as it takes. When I do the wrong thing, He gives me the chance to fix it. He knows my heart. Notice I said "when," not "if," because there's always gonna be a "when."

For years, there were things I wanted to do, but I didn't have the time or money, I thought. I always told myself that when I win the lottery, I'm going to quit my job, donate to certain charities, volunteer at the church, and many other things. I had all these dreams, and they were keeping me from living my life. It was always "someday."

Then one day I heard the Holy Spirit say, "Start where you are." What a great idea. So, I started to do what I could when I could. It wasn't a lot, but it was a start. What I'm doing now isn't as much as I'd like, but it's more than what I used to do, and not as much as I'm going to do. I think about how my praying in the shower has turned into a prayer life that I never thought possible, all because I started where I was. If there's something you really want to do but you're waiting for *your* "someday," make your someday today and start where you are. If you love babies but don't have any, go to a hospital or your church's nursery on Sundays and ask if they need help rocking the babies. If you want to give to a charity but you don't have lots of money, give a dollar. Just think, if 999 other people give a dollar, and who's to say they aren't, you could be a part of donating $1,000 to your favorite charity. What is it you're waiting for? Start where you are.

I have come to realize that living in the center of God's will means not being selfish with my time but being generous with the time and abundance God has blessed me with. I've noticed the more I'm in His will, the more time and abundance I have.

God predestined our lives, but He will not force His will on us because He has given us all free will. God is patiently waiting for us to ask Him what His will is for our lives. I promise you He won't keep it a secret. But once you ask, be ready. God loves joyful obedience. Ask Him every day to show you what He wants you to do that day. Then listen, be available, and do what He says.

I have proven God so many times that I don't have to anymore. He's faithful. He has always been faithful. He always will be faithful. He can't *not* be faithful.

Obey God and leave all the consequences to Him.

Fruit of the Spirit

The fruit of the Spirit is love, joy, peace, patience, kindness, faithfulness, gentleness, goodness and self-control. It's not always easy for these virtues to be seen in me, but I'm working on it, constantly. God filled me with them. It's my job for people to be able to see them.

I used to think peace was the best virtue. There is no way to explain His peace when you have it. I've tried. It's literally impossible. Could be why the

Bible explains it as, "…the peace of God, which surpasses all understanding…", Philippians 4:7. *Could* be. Total peace, no matter what is happening in my life, is the most awesome feeling in the world.

But then I think about love. The way I feel about my husband, family, and friends. Living without people to love, and who love you, is just sad. First Corinthians 13:13 says, "And now abide faith, hope, love, these three; but the greatest of these is love." There is no greater feeling than to love and be loved.

Then there's the joy I have when I do an act of kindness for someone. I have never been able to do something for someone else when God did not bless me more than the person I was trying to bless. You can't outgive God. I always thought that meant financially, but I have learned that it is with everything I do. Try it. Do any act of kindness and then watch for it. God will bless you. And He will bless you in ways you do not even know are possible.

And then there's patience. To have patience with others (like a spouse or parent), while I'm driving, standing in line, or one of the other 1,000 reasons I need patience, is a Godsend.

Love, joy, peace, etc., they all put a smile on my face. I'm glad I don't have to pick just one.

Obey God and leave all the consequences to Him.

Filled with the Holy Spirit

Life Principle No. 22: *To walk in the Spirit is to obey the initial promptings of the Spirit.*

When we are saved, the Holy Spirit comes to live in us. He is our Helper. Remember, He is also part of the Trinity: God the Father, God the Son and God the Holy Spirit. So, actually, God comes to live inside of us.

Walking by the Spirit is to be led by the Spirit. The result is to bear the fruit of the Spirit which shows how our lives are being changed from old to new, becoming more Christlike in every area of our lives. The goal is to have a heart transformation. To no longer have worldly desires, but to have a new heart and mind that continually seeks to do the will of God.

When we follow the promptings of the Holy Spirit, we bear fruit. We can't do God's will without the Holy Spirit. He knows our lives completely from the moment we're conceived through eternity. He knows God's plan and purpose for us, for each day of our lives.

John 16:13 says, "...He will guide you into all truth; for He will not speak on His own authority, but whatever He hears He will speak; and He will tell you things to come."

He is always encouraging us to act how Jesus would act, to say what He would say, or do what He would do, in any given moment. God wants us to trust the Holy Spirit to be our daily Guide. The Holy Spirit guides us onto the right path for us to walk and convicts us of our sin when we stray from that path. He also teaches us how to apply God's Word to our daily lives. We must learn to say yes to the Spirit when He prompts us to take a certain action or say a certain word. For it is the Holy Spirit who helps believers discern between what is true and what is not.

The Holy Spirit gives us that extra on-the-spot sense of discernment we need to make both big and small decisions. He isn't here to help with certain areas of our lives, He is here to help in *all* areas of our lives. From the major to the minor.

Here's a sample of one of my *very* minors. I bought a card for a baby shower. I placed a picture of my back-ordered gift inside the card. As I was getting ready to seal it (I always lick envelopes, because I like the taste of the glue) I heard the Holy Spirit say, "Don't seal it. You'll have to open it back up." So, as I was disobediently sealing it I was picturing myself trying to neatly slice the card open. And the next day, when I found out the gift was now discontinued, I was not surprised when the envelope ripped and I had to go out and buy another card. Hmmm. Obey the initial promptings of the Holy Spirit. I guess God really does help with *everything*!!! What I enjoy most about that story is the fact that I knew when the Holy Spirit was prompting me. What I don't like is the fact that I didn't obey His prompting. And I knew better! I'm pretty much at a point where I always know. I just don't always obey. OBVIOUSLY! Life sure is a lot easier when I do. And less expensive.

The best way I can describe the promptings of the Holy Spirit is like this: it's like having an idea, but it's not my idea. I'll just get a thought all of a sudden. It may be to call someone, pray for someone, go somewhere or do something. One time I heard, clean the house. I did. I got unexpected company. Sometimes it's reminders. A lot of times, it's reminders. I'll be at the grocery store and God will remind me to get something I forgot to put on my list. Or I'll be driving, and He'll remind me of somewhere I need to go. I'm not trying to think of these things. They just pop in my head.

Like when I'm getting ready to go somewhere. Instead of having the thought, "I think I'll turn the porch light on", it's like someone saying, "Turn the porch light on." I use this as an example because I have come home to a dark porch too many times. Every time I heard the prompting but responded with, "Oh, I'll be home way before dark." Yeah. No.

The husband of a friend of mine was thinking about one of his friends and couldn't get him off his mind. He decided to call that person and found out he had just been to his father's funeral. That's the Holy Spirit. It warms my heart to know I have friends who follow the promptings of the Holy Spirit. Those promptings are like a voice in your head, but it's not audible. It's like what some people call a "gut feeling." One of my friends calls it "my gut, my God."

One day I had six errands to run, and I wanted to meet up with one of my friends for a few minutes. I could have either started my errands on

West Lane or Lower Sacramento Road. I decided to go West Lane, but I got a restless spirit and knew God was trying to tell me something. I stopped the car and said, "Okay, God, which way." Immediately, Lower Sac popped into my head. I *obeyed*!!! YAY!!! When I only had two places left to go, I called my friend and asked if she could meet me at some point. She said she couldn't because she had too many errands and she was on her way to Costco. Guess where I was headed when I called her? Correct. Costco. If I had gone the other way, my second stop would have been Costco, and I would have been long gone by the time she got there. I just knew that was God loving me. Being able to visit my precious friend was God's blessing to me for obedience. Everything went perfectly that day. Actually, every day that I stay in contact with God and follow the promptings of the Holy Spirit are perfect days. The only bad days I have are the ones I try and do on my own.

God wants to be part of our daily life. And He's good at it. So, every day I ask God to make me sensitive to His voice so I will know and follow the promptings of the Holy Spirit the second I am prompted.

Obey God and leave all the consequences to Him.

Did You Know That...

King David was an adulterer, Satan quoted scripture, Moses was a murderer, and Peter, one of

Jesus' disciples, denied knowing Jesus *three times*? I *know*!

Let's start with King David. He saw Bathsheba. He slept with Bathsheba while her husband, Uriah, was away in battle. Bathsheba got pregnant. David had Uriah sent home from battle so he could sleep with Bathsheba, ASAP. But Uriah would not enjoy the comforts of home, because his friends were still in battle. So, David had him sent back to the front line so he would be killed. And he was. David married Bathsheba. Soooo, I guess David was an adulterer *and* a murderer. And yes, this is the same man who pleased God so much that He made him a king. God *always* loves the person. Just not the sin. God knows our heart.

Even being loved by God as much as David was didn't give him a free pass for his disobedience. There were terrible consequences, including the death of the child born to him and Bathsheba. But David repented, and when they had another child, God made *him* a king. Remember King Solomon, the wisest, richest king that ever lived? That would be him.

Now to Moses. One day Moses saw a man beating a fellow Israelite, and when he thought no one was looking, he killed the man and hid his body. This is the same Moses God used to lead the children of Israel out of Egypt and to the Promised Land. The Ten Commandments guy. Sadly, Moses wasn't able to enter the Promised Land. One act of disobedience kept him from getting in. What could he possibly have done for God not to let him into the Promised Land, you ask? Well, I'll tell you. At one point along the journey God had Moses strike a rock for water to come out. Later, God told Moses to *speak* to a rock for water to come out. But Moses was so frustrated with the way the Israelites were behaving (badly) that he struck the rock instead of speaking to it. That was all it took. So, at 120 years old and in perfect health Moses stood on a hill and looked over into the Promised Land, never stepping foot in it. And then he died. How sad.

Then there's Peter, the disciple Jesus called the "Rock." Just before Jesus was taken away to be crucified, He said to Peter, "'Assuredly, I say to you that this night, before the rooster crows, you will deny Me three times.' Peter said to Him, 'Even if I have to die with you, I will not deny You!' and so said all the disciples," Matthew 26:34-35.

Matthew 26:70, Peter denied knowing Jesus. Verse 72, Peter denied knowing Jesus. Verse 74, Peter denied knowing Jesus. Immediately, a rooster crowed. Verse 75, "And Peter remembered the word of Jesus who had said to him, 'Before the rooster crows, you will deny Me three times.' Peter went out and wept bitterly."

Would you pick these guys to be a king, a disciple, and someone to lead a nation? God did. And He can use you too. I forgot to mention Paul. He went from persecuting Christians to writing 13 books in the Bible.

And if there is no God and the Bible is just a book, why was Satan quoting scripture...*to Jesus*? In Luke 4:10-11, Satan quotes scripture from Psalm

91:11-12. Satan starts with, "For it is written:". Apparently, Satan knows the Bible, and *better* than *I* do. Hmmmm.

Satan does exist. He knows there's a God, a Heaven and a hell. Revelation 12:7-12 talks about it. In essence, war broke out in Heaven and Michael and his angels fought with Satan and his angels. Satan and his angels lost and were cast out of Heaven. Satan deceives the world. Verse 12, "Woe to the inhabitants of the earth and the sea! For the devil has come down to you, having great wrath, because he knows that he has a short time." Satan knows where he is spending eternity, and he wants to take as many of us with him as he can. Our mind is also Satan's playground. Don't let him get a foothold.

Remember what God allowed him to do to Job? Satan picked Job to torture because he was such an upright, godly man. Satan is pure evil.

Satan originated in Heaven. He knows he's spending eternity in hell. Since he can't go back to Heaven, he doesn't want us to go there either.

To have been in Heaven and then thrown out, no wonder he's mad. I guess it's true…misery loves company.

James 2:19 says, "You believe that there is one God. You do well. Even the demons believe…and tremble!"

Obey God and leave all the consequences to Him.

Prayer and Praise

Life Lesson on page 607 of my Bible says, "Every breath we take is really the breath of God. It belongs to Him, and He can take it back at any time. So, let us use our breath to glorify and praise Him, so long as we have it." Sometimes I'll just stop and say, "Thank you, God. The praise and glory for everything good and right in our lives and in this world are Yours alone." That's it.

My morning prayer time is my favorite time of day. On the days I don't take time to pray, I can tell a difference. My day becomes more of a struggle than a joy. There is nothing like starting your day on your knees before God. I can just feel Him with me all day. It gives me such peace to feel God's presence.

Because I believe in the Trinity (God, Jesus and the Holy Spirit are separate, but One), sometimes I pray to God, sometimes Jesus, and when I just don't know what to say, I ask the Holy Spirit to intercede in prayer for me. I close my prayers by saying, "In Jesus' precious name I pray." I added "precious" because He is. Just doing that has made a difference for me. Think about what you're saying. Prayer is a very powerful and amazing thing. We have all of God's power available to us at any given time. It can be overwhelming when you think about it. All of Heaven and earth are available to you when you ask. Why wouldn't you?

Our prayers move God into action. God doesn't need our prayers. He wants them. He wants us to be in constant communication with Him. That's how we keep an intimate relationship with Him.

Whenever I pray for something or someone, I know there are three possible answers: yes, no, and wait.

When it is His will and the time is right, the answer is yes. Sometimes my prayers are answered while I am still on my knees praying. There's been healing, a job for someone, and even attitude adjustments (mostly mine). Do you have any idea how awesome it is to have a prayer answered *while* you are still praying? I love it! I highly recommend finding out for yourself.

At times I've thought the answer was "no," but it turned out to be "wait." I love "wait" answers because God's perfect timing is always worth the wait. He is either preparing me for the blessing because I'm not ready for it, or He may be increasing my trust in Him by having me wait on Him.

Sometimes the answer is "no." I have come to like "no" answers as well. That means whatever I was praying for would not have been good for me or the person I was praying for. God protects us out of love.

I read somewhere, "If you worry, pray. If you pray, don't worry." I can't think of anything I worry about anymore. Now, when something comes up, I say, "God, take it." Then I smile, knowing He's got it, and I don't have a care in the world. The closer you get to God, the easier it is to let go.

Obey God and leave all the consequences

to Him.

It's the Everything

Often, I just stop and say, "God, thanks for the everything." Because it's not just one thing with God. It's the everything. When I start my day with God, ask Him what He wants me to do that day and listen for Him to tell me, I am constantly saying, "Thanks for the everything." Because those days are the best days. They're the ones that don't go anything like I planned but are filled with things I don't even know are possible. I just love that.

I don't worry about the things I *thought* I was supposed to do and didn't get done. If God wants me to do them, they'll get done when *He* says so. Fine by me. God is in control. I'm worry free.

I previously mentioned that God is in every area of my life, from the major to the minor. I gave you an example of the minor but have been racking my brain trying to think of a major. I guess this next story is a biggie, but, to me, it's all part of the adventure.

During the writing of this book, I found two new breast lumps. I had an ultrasound, but it was indeterminate. A biopsy was scheduled. I asked my praying family members and friends to pray for me. I asked God to dissolve or just get rid of the lumps. The one the doctor thought might be fluid, I asked God to have that one be fluid and just have them needle aspirate it. I also asked God for it to be so painless I wouldn't need any medication afterwards, and that I would have no recovery time. Like always, my prayer was, "Fix it, God, just fix it."

Even though I was trusting for complete healing, I knew God might have another adventure for me. I was prepared for Him to have me show others that my faith and trust were real no matter what was happening in my life. I was even ready to go home to Heaven if that's what God wanted. Death is not the end, but a new beginning. However, if a person dies without being saved, I believe it's a tragedy. I'm looking forward to Heaven and I'm not afraid of dying but I would like to stay here with my husband and loved ones for many more years.

I went to my appointment early and read my Bible. I was reminding myself of God's faithfulness, His love for me, His ability to heal me if He chose to, and His desire to have me completely dependent on Him for everything. I was resting in His loving arms. I kept repeating, "Fix it, God" and "Take it, God", because I had faith that He would. And that relaxed me. I had His perfect peace that surpasses all human understanding. I thanked Him for every next second with Him, and for the awesome adventure that we were on together. I was ready for anything. And I knew, no matter what, He had me.

I went in for my biopsy and found out they were going to biopsy three lumps, not two. I told the girl who was starting the ultrasound not to be surprised if she couldn't find the lumps, as I had asked God to get rid of them. So, I was not surprised when she said she could not find two of the lumps. They were just gone. The doctor doing the biopsy could not find them either. He then told me he was pretty sure the solid lump was fluid, and he was going to needle aspirate it; but if it wasn't fluid, then he would biopsy it.

He was able to needle aspirate the lump and told me I was good to go. Everything looked fine. No pain, no recovery time; sounds like answered prayer to me. God is very good to me. "God, thanks for the everything."

Then there's the time I had to have a tooth dug out. The dentist said I might have problems with the tooth next to it, and he was pretty sure I was going to have a hole in my sinus when he was done. I wasn't worried. I asked God to make it go easy peasy, no hole in my sinus and no other tooth problems. The procedure couldn't have gone better.

I love the way God works. My sister was in town one day and I wanted to see her, but I had a previous commitment. I thought I would be done in plenty of time, but I wasn't. She called me and said she was heading back home. I still had about an hour to work. She said, "Next time." And I said, "Yeah, next time." I was heartbroken. I finished an hour later and called her just to talk. To my delight, she was still around, and I was able to have dinner with her. Obey God….

One evening I had tickets to a crab feed. Earlier that day I had thought about a girl I'd been meaning to call for a couple years. Yes, years. I made up my mind to call her the next day. I wasn't going to put it off any longer. I walked into the crab feed and almost ran right into her. I like obedience. I had spent time with God, read my Bible, listened for a bit that morning, and had another perfect day.

One day I was in line at Peet's Coffee. Two women came in behind me who were meeting the lady in front of me. They were talking to each other about what they were going to order, so I told the ladies behind me to get in front of me. When they finished placing their orders, they gave me a coupon for a dollar off my drink. Do what's right and everything else will follow.

Another day, I went to lunch with my girlfriends and one of them had her first-grade-age nephew with her. We all got cookies with our lunch, and I gave him mine. I thought he might enjoy having an extra cookie. After lunch I went up to the counter to buy a cookie to take home. One of my precious friends told me she wanted to buy me a cookie. After losing the argument, I agreed. She bought one for herself as well. The cookies were about three times bigger than the ones we got with lunch. I gave her half of mine, and she gave me half of hers.

God works like this: I gave away a small cookie. In return, I got a cookie three times the size of the one I gave away, *and* I had two different kinds to enjoy. God always blesses us with more, and better.

And then there are those things that simply amaze me. One of the times my sister and I were babysitting for the Hinchmans, we fed the kids Froot Loops for their bedtime snack. Unfortunately, we didn't know it was going to be their breakfast the next morning. All these years later, I still felt so bad for Mr. Hinchman who had to run out the next morning at 6 a.m. to buy more cereal. Who knew people actually eat cereal for breakfast? That's a bedtime snack.

Well, on December 13, 2010, I saw Mr. and Mrs. Hinchman. I hadn't seen them in 38 years. I was able to apologize, in person, and tell them how bad I still felt about using the Froot Loops for their kids' bedtime snack. Mr. Hinchman said, "Huh? What Froot Loops? What are you talking about?" This was something I thought about so often and he didn't even remember. Now he'll probably never forget. This makes me think about all the other memories I need to let go of. Things that still bother me but hopefully nobody else remembers. I think I'm too sensitive.

We also talked about the night my sister and I had to let them know we couldn't babysit for them because of "The Divorce." That night, Mrs. Hinchman stopped what she was doing, raising *five* children, and came over to make sure we were okay. Funny how I remembered the Froot Loops and had forgotten that. I think I'll keep that memory now and let the Froot Loops go. It's time. I love the way God works.

Obey God and leave all the consequences to Him.

Be the One Who...

...takes a minute to call your spouse just to say, "I love you."

...takes time to call your parent just to say, "I love you." (Because one day you won't be able to)

...takes five seconds a day to kneel down and say, "Thank you, God. I love you."

...repeats Bible verses during the day.

...says hello to everyone you make eye contact with.

...always has a smile on your face.

...has a heart bent toward God.

...turns the radio off in the car and talks to God. Or, better yet, just listens.

...asks God to show you what you can do for Him each day, and then thank Him for enabling and equipping you to do it.

Obey God and leave all the consequences to Him.

Our Purpose for Being

We were created by God for fellowship with Him and to glorify Him in all that we do. He will take care of the rest. He always planned to.

I used to think how lucky I was when something good would happen to me. But now I know there is no luck. It's God. It always has been, and it always will be.

If you're not saved, then it's Satan giving you a false sense of happiness, because Satan is the great deceiver. He wants your soul, but God wants it too. Be very careful to whom you give it.

Every so often you hear someone say, "There's just something missing in my life." If they're not saved, it's God. Without God in their life there is a huge hole. Nothing they do, say, buy, smoke or drink will ever fill it. If they are saved, the only thing missing is a closer relationship with God. God fills the empty parts. If you need to, ask God to fill you up.

God wants very much to have an intimate relationship with us. We should want that just as much. When I let go and let God control every area of my life I am at total peace. How great is that? That peace is not something I can achieve apart from God, no matter how hard I try. I cannot find peace in the world. Peace is another awesome gift from God.

We weren't created to live willy-nilly, doing what we want, when we want, and thinking everything should be about our happiness. God made Adam and Eve for fellowship. He made them in His image so He could talk to and walk with them in the Garden of Eden. "Then God said, 'Let Us make man in Our image, according to Our likeness…'", Genesis 1:26. "And they heard the sound of the Lord God walking in the garden in the cool of the day…", Genesis 3:8. Imagine God leaving Heaven to come visit you. If they had only known what an awesome thing that was. Instead, it was just a normal, probably everyday occurrence for them.

God provided all their needs. They had no

worries or problems. There wasn't even going to be any pain in childbirth. Everything was perfect in the garden, and it would have stayed that way if they had not sinned. They could have lived forever. No, really, I'm not making this up. We are going to have eternal bodies when we get to Heaven, so that was my first clue. And then, Genesis 5:25-26 says, "Methuselah lived one hundred and eighty-seven years and begot Lamech. After he begot Lamech, Methuselah lived seven hundred and eighty-two years, and had sons and daughters." So, obviously, our bodies could last longer than our current lifespan. Fun Fact: When you hear it said that someone, or something, is as old as Methuselah, it's this guy.

During the writing of this, something caught my attention that I had never noticed before. I have read the following verse at least 20 times, if not more, and in my mind I had always combined the tree of life with the tree of the knowledge of good and evil. But they are two totally different trees.

Genesis 2:9 says, "And out of the ground the Lord God made every tree grow that is pleasant to the sight and good for food. The tree of life was also in the midst of the garden, and the tree of the knowledge of good and evil."

Genesis 2:16-17 says, "And the Lord God commanded man, saying, 'Of every tree of the garden you may freely eat; but of the tree of the knowledge of good and evil you shall not eat, for in the day that you eat of it you shall surely die.'" So, as long as they were eating from the tree of life they would never die? Sounds like.

After Adam and Eve sinned by eating the fruit from the tree of the knowledge of good and evil, Genesis 3:22 says, "Then the Lord God said, 'Behold, the man has become like one of Us, to know good and evil. And now, lest he put out his hand and take also of the tree of life, and eat, and live forever...'" (there it is, I didn't make it up), verse 24, "So He drove out the man; and He placed cherubim at the east of the garden of Eden, and a flaming sword which turned every way, to guard the way to the tree of life."

Adam and Eve blew it. Their best, and only, friend was God. *GOD*! They ate from a tree that enabled them to live forever. FOR EVER!! Everything was perfect. Yet they sinned. Not much hope for us not sinning after that, is there? And, yes, Adam threw Eve under the bus when God asked him if he had eaten from the tree. Genesis 3:12, "Then the man said, 'The woman whom You gave to be with me, she gave me of the tree, and I ate.'" Sounds like he's also blaming God. He ate the fruit of his own God-given free will, and then literally blames everyone else for his actions. If there had been more people on this earth, he probably would have blamed them as well. I guess we've always had a problem taking responsibility for our own actions. To this day, we are living with the consequences of that one sinful act.

I figured out the chicken and the egg one too. The chicken came first. Genesis 1:24, "Then God said, 'Let the earth bring forth the <u>living creature</u>

according to its kind: cattle and creeping thing and beast of the earth, each according to its kind'; and it was so." No mention of eggs. Besides, if the egg came first, there wouldn't have been a chicken to sit on it until it hatched.

See, everything you want to know is somewhere in the Bible.

Obey God and leave all the consequences to Him.

The Miracle of God

The fact that God *is,* is a miracle. What made God? Think about it. There was absolutely nothing *but* God. How was God formed if there was nothing to make Him? Only two things keep me from going crazy wondering about this. First, I'm just so grateful that He *is,* that I don't care how He *got* here. Second, all will be made known to us when we get to Heaven. Good enough for me.

God knows everything from the beginning of time through eternity. He even knows everything we're going to do or say before we do or say it. Sooo, if we ever think we're getting away with something, we're not.

God is love. God is the creator of all, but mostly, God is love. First John 4:8 says, "He who does not love does not know God, for God is love." Verse 16 says, "And we have known and believed the love that God has for us. God is love, and he who abides in love abides in God, and God in him." Verse 19, "We love Him because He first loved us."

How did God come to be with the awesome attributes that He has? That's another thing that I wonder about. But, again, I'm just so grateful that He *is*.

In John 20:29, Jesus tells one of His disciples, "Thomas, because you have seen Me, you have believed. Blessed *are* those who have not seen and *yet* have believed." That would be people like me; and I am *so* blessed. Fun Fact: We get the term "Doubting Thomas" from this guy because he wouldn't believe that Jesus had really risen from the dead until he saw Him in person.

Obey God and leave all the consequences to Him.

Saved by Grace with Love and Mercy

This is what I believe, and why. Ephesians 2:8-9 says, "For by grace you have been saved through faith, and that not of yourselves; it is the gift of God, not of works, lest anyone should boast."

Romans 6:23 says, "For the wages of sin is death, but the gift of God is eternal life in Christ Jesus our Lord."

John 14:6, "Jesus said to him, 'I am the way, the truth, and the life. No one comes to the Father except through Me.'"

I believe Jesus died on the cross for our salvation, the forgiveness of our sins; for which *everyone* is welcome to receive. And then He rose again on the third day and now sits at the right hand of God in Heaven. Like the Bible says in

Romans 6:10, "For the death that He died, He died to sin once for all…." He took my place on the cross. He took yours too.

In Mark 14:36, Jesus says, "Abba, Father, all things are possible for You. Take this cup away from Me; nevertheless, not what I will, but what You will." Jesus knew what was coming, the horrors of being beaten and nailed to a cross. And yet, that's not what He was asking God to deliver Him from. He was willing to do that for us because that's how much He loves us. But He knew the moment He became the sin of the world—our sin—He would be separated from His Father—and our Father—God. And He knew there is nothing worse than being without God. Even being crucified on a cross was not as bad as being separated from God. At any given time, He could have called on more than 12 legions of angels to come help Him. But He didn't. That's how much He loves us…*all* of us. I want the way I live my life to be a thank you to Him every day. Because just *saying* thank you doesn't even begin to be enough. Jesus allowed himself to be separated from God so we would never have to be. That's love. And it's unconditional.

Because I believe that Jesus died for my salvation, I am now a saint in the kingdom of Heaven. A child of God. Even though I am still *in* the world, I am not *of* the world. All that I am, and all that I have, comes from God. As long as I keep my focus on God, the world can fall apart, but I'll be okay. His promise to me, "…I will uphold you with My righteous right hand," Isaiah, 41:10.

The ways of God start with His love. And because of His love for me, He abundantly blesses me with His mercy and grace. And that's just for starters.

Mercy is God *not* giving me what I deserve.

Grace is God giving me what I *don't* deserve.

How blessed I am to know that I'm going to Heaven and that God loves me, no matter what. And that His love, mercy, and grace are never ending. God loves me so much that He gave me my salvation as a gift, thru His Son Jesus. And if that was all God gave me, that would be more than enough. But God being God, that's only the beginning.

Obey God and leave all the consequences to Him.

Faith

Hebrews 11:1 says, "Faith is being sure of what we hope for and certain of what we do not see."

I *am* sure of what I hope for…there is a God. And I'm *certain* of what I do not see…God.

Trust

Proverbs 3:5-6 says, "Trust in the Lord with all your heart and lean not on your own understanding. In all your ways acknowledge Him and He will direct your path."

If God is your co-pilot, switch places.

Fortunately, I learned a long time ago not to

expect anything from anyone other than God. People will always disappoint at one time or another. Not always intentionally, but it will happen. God, however, is as good as His word. Psalm 62:5 says, "My soul, wait silently for God alone, for my expectation is from Him." "It is better to trust in the Lord than to put confidence in man," Psalm 118:8.

Obedience

Isaiah 30:21 says, "Your ears shall hear a word behind you, saying, 'This is the way, walk in it,' whenever you turn to the right hand or whenever you turn to the left." Listen for His voice and you *will* hear it.

God blesses our obedience more than we ask for, expect, or deserve. You can never win by disobeying God, and never lose by obeying Him.

Obey God and leave all the consequences to Him.

My Life Today

My life is far from perfect. I wouldn't want it to be. Although, a little closer would be nice. And I work on it...daily.

Unfortunately, we need adversity in our lives to keep us close to God. I say unfortunately because that means I'm drifting away from God. It's not the adversity that I mind so much; it's the not-being-so-close-to-God-you-can't-tell-us-apart part. These days, adversity usually comes in the form of my husband. He can make me crazier than my dead Aunt Sue. But he's my bridge to a deeper relationship with God. He gets me going, and I run to God. These are the "change me, change him, just FIX IT, PLEASE!" prayers. Remember? The ones that end with an adjusted attitude—mine. One day I told Gary, "You sure are keeping me close to God lately." He said, "You're welcome." The neighbors could hear us laughing. God knows what each of us needs. Apparently, I need Gary. If truth be told, I'm his adversity. I can admit it. I can be a little much at times. Don't get me wrong, I'm *very* glad God always has an adversity bridge when I need one. I just wish I didn't have to cross it so often.

It's beyond my comprehension how God can still love me, but I know He does. He shows me just how much, every day of my life. To this day, it breaks my heart to know I still grieve God's Spirit at times. But I know no matter what I do, God still loves me unconditionally.

I'm at a point where I'm pretty much in tune with the Holy Spirit; but I still ask God to enable me to discern His voice the second He prompts me. Now, if I would just follow His promptings every time. That pesky free will can get me in more trouble.

I have the same problems, worries, fears, and anxieties everyone else has. I just don't hang on to them anymore. God promised me that if I lived my life in obedience to Him, He would be faithful and take these things from me. And He does. Every time. He doesn't lie. Now I automatically give God a problem the second I get it, at least 99% of the time. Every once in a while, it takes me a couple minutes—or days—to remember to let go. Drives my husband crazy that I don't worry about anything anymore. Drives me crazy that he still does—though not as much as he used to. Okay, there's still one thing I stress over, but there's a fine line between the right amount of mayo in tuna and, oops, sorry honey. With God, everything clicks, He makes the lights turn green.

Here's a shocker. I got baptized again. I *know*! I've just been so grateful to God for my amazing life that I wanted to show Him by re-dedicating my life to Him. Another way of saying thank you. My pastor at the time, had a river running alongside his home. So, I was baptized by Pastors Dennis Baskin and Rob Bline in an ice-cold river. And it was perfect.

Obey God and leave all the consequences to Him.

Let Go, Let God

Just think where I'd be if I had never given God control of my job. I have no doubt I would still be working in escrow, still having headaches and chest pains, still living a life filled with worry, fear, stress and anxiety at work and home. But my life is so different now. I never thought in a million years my life would be like this. I didn't even know it was an option.

We were created by God to glorify Him. We can't do that if our focus is not on Him. He never planned for us to be in control. God loves us so much He gave us free will; but He would like very much for us to choose His will over ours. Test Him if you want. I did. He expects it. Give Him one thing. It can be little or big. See what He does with it. I promise you, before long you'll be giving Him your problems the second they come up—or wishing you had, like I still do. When we surrender everything to God we are untying His hands and enabling Him to take over.

I used to wonder what my life would have been like had my parents not divorced or if I had made different choices. But, instead of regretting my life's choices, I've decided to be grateful for what they have taught me. Thank you, Stacey, for reminding me of that. I have compassion for those I might not have had compassion for had I not personally experienced what they were going through.

Instead of focusing on the negative, I choose to look for the positives. Because of my parents' divorce and change of high schools, I have the most loving, kind, generous husband. I have priceless friends who are friends for life. And if you're as blessed as I am, divorce only gives you more people to love and that love you. I have the best-ever mom, dad, and stepfather. And instead of one terrific sister, I have four. Just because the parents divorce doesn't mean the siblings have to. I also have two wonderful brothers. One of which is already enjoying the presence of God. I absolutely couldn't love them more if I tried. All of them are amazing blessings from God.

My world didn't end after the divorce like I thought it had; it just went in a different direction.

Obey God and leave all the consequences to Him.

No Bible, No God; Know Bible, Know God

I know I've repeated some things. I thought it was age, but I checked. They were worth repeating.

I also know I have quoted a lot of scripture. But that was for a very good reason. To have a relationship with Jesus and draw closer to God, we have to get to know them. The only way to do that is to read the Bible and let them tell us about themselves. And the Holy Spirit, who lives in us, gives us discernment so we can understand what they are saying.

Trust the Holy Spirit to be your daily Guide. We are to be diligent in seeking His guidance, asking for it, watching for it, anticipating it, and receiving it. Hebrews 11:6 says, "God is a rewarder of those who diligently seek Him." The only way to know God is to know the Bible.

Obey God and leave all the consequences to Him.

May the Lord Bless You and Keep You

When it's all over, I want to hear God say to me, "Well done, good and faithful servant," Matthew

25:21. How about you?

My prayer is for each of you to have complete trust and faith in God, and to be joyfully obedient in all things. Then you too will be thanking God every day for being the Most Blessed person in the world.

I leave you with this blessing from Numbers 6:24-26:

> *"The Lord bless you and keep you;*
> *The Lord make His face shine upon you,*
> *And be gracious to you;*
> *The Lord lift up His countenance upon you,*
> *And give you peace."*

Jesus, the ULTIMATE SACRIFICE

Each morning I wake, my first thought is of You,
My only constant, faithful and true.
How You must love a sinner like me,
One who helped nail Your hands to a tree.
You left Heaven and Glory
To come tell Your story.
Before You came You knew the price;
Your life would be the ULTIMATE SACRIFICE.
This life You began as a babe in a manger;
To this world You were but a stranger.
For thirty-three years You stayed in this land;
Though constantly tempted, You were a sinless man.
Of salvation You told, little praise You received;
For this gift made so easy, have faith and believe.
Eternal life You said would be ours,
But You would be the One with the scars.
You became our sin, hung and died on a cross;
For without Your death, we ALL would be lost.
Your work on earth done, Heaven's gates opened wide,
To welcome You back to Glory, and Your Father's Right
Side.

by
Lori Polk

Do you have a relationship with God?

The Bible says:

> God loves you and wants a relationship with you (Romans 5:8; 1 John 4:10).
>
> God sent His Son to earth as a man—Jesus—to die on the cross and pay the penalty for your sins (Isaiah 53:6; Romans 6:23).
>
> You can become a child of God by accepting Jesus' gift of salvation in faith and placing your trust in Him (John 1:12; Romans 10:9-10).

Would you like to know God?

> Below is a suggested prayer of salvation, but feel free to pray your own words as you talk to God.
>
> > *Heavenly Father, I confess that I have sinned against You and need your salvation. Please forgive me. I receive Jesus Christ as my Lord and Savior, fully trusting in the work He accomplished on the cross on my behalf. Thank You for saving me, accepting me, and adopting me into Your family. Help me to walk in close step with you. Amen*

If you became a follower of Jesus today, you've made the most important decision of your life, one that can never be taken away from you (Ephesians 1:13-14). For more information, please visit In Touch Ministries at intouch.org.

I'll see you in Heaven!

www.ingramcontent.com/pod-product-compliance
Lightning Source LLC
Chambersburg PA
CBHW071829020426
42331CB00007B/1666